KU-175-504

Montana!

A Photographic Celebration

Volume 1

by Rick Graetz
Photography by Rick Graetz and others

Published by Rick Graetz—Northern Rockies Publishing
through
Montana Magazine—American Geographic Publishing
Helena, Montana U.S.A.

Photographers contributing work to this issue:

Pete and Alice Bengeyfield
Tim Christie
Michael Crummett
Tom Dietrich
Christopher Dwyer
Doug Dye
Tim Egan
Diane Ensign
Phil Farnes
Michael Francis
Susie Graetz
Lisa Hale
Kent Krone
Neal and Mary Jane Mishler
Pat O'Hara
Rob Outlaw
John Reddy
Conrad Rowe
Dean Sauskojus
Del Siegle
Keith Szafranski
Larry S. Thompson
Bruce Weide
George Wuerthner
Garry Wunderwald

ISBN 0-938314-60-2 (P)
Design by Linda Collins
Photographic selection and consulting by Susie Graetz
Printed in Korea by Dong-A Printing Co.
© Rick Graetz 1988

About the Author

Publishling executive, businessman, mountainman environmentalist, photographer, civic and political leader; just a few of the labels that describe Rick Graetz of Helena, Montana.

Rick is the publisher of MONTANA MAGAZINE and the American Geographic Series, some of the most beautiful state oriented publications in the nation, and part owner of, and a guide for High Country Adventures, a backpacking and mountaineering outfitting service.

Rick's scenic photos have appeared in books, calendars, catalogs, maps, annual reports, magazines, brochures and on the walls of many business and government offices. His talks and slide shows are in demand all over Montana, and at many outdoor and business meetings throughout the nation.

Whenever he can find the time, Rick writes freelance articles to accompany his photography and is the author of several books, including *Montana's Bob Marshall Country, Vietnam: Opening Doors to the World* and co-author of Montana Is. He has climbed and skied mountains and floated rivers throughout North America, including Alaska and the Yukon, South America, Hawaii and Asia, and has scaled more than 250 Montana mountains.

Introduction

During the course of 18 years our company has published thousands of Montana photographs in *Montana Magazine, The Montana Geographic Series* and our many other publications. The high-quality work submitted keeps increasing, making bi-monthly photo selection for *Montana Magazine* difficult. With limited space for color, much of the fine photography sent to us goes unpublished.

With *Montana! A Photographic Celebration, Volume 1*, we hope to commence a regular publication that will enable us to display more frequently an additional 150 to 200 of the very best of Montana photography—images depicting our magnificent scenery, wildlife and people at work and play.

The goal of each edition will be to ensure that all areas of Montana are represented—from the snowcapped western peaks to the subtle beauty of Montana east of the mountains.

The enthusiasm for Montana is intense and perhaps this explains the abundance of photographs. Through *American Geographic Publishing* we produce books for many states. And although we conduct a wide search for photography for each area of the country, the number of people taking Montana pictures, and the amount of photos available, far exceed anywhere else. The interest in buying Montana books is also great. Our sales for Montana publications per capita are more than for any other state.

The ingredients that cause this love affair with one state are many. I can promise you we'll show off the results that come from the camera in superbly produced books.

Rick Graetz
Prickly Pear Valley, Montana
September 1988

Front cover photo: North Fork of the Flathead Valley. DOUG DYE
Back cover, Top row left to right: Bighorn Canyon. RICK GRAETZ
Young cowboy, Cjay Clark. SUSIE GRAETZ
Canadian Geese at sunrise. NEAL AND MARY JANE MISHLER
Bottom row left to right: Misson Mountains. DIANE ENSIGN
Cottontail. TIM CHRISTIE
Weathered wood and wildflowers. JOHN REDDY
Title page: Sunrise, McDonald Lake, Glacier National Park. PETE AND ALICE BENGEYFIELD
Facing page: The Danaher Meadows in the Bob Marshall Wilderness. RICK GRAETZ
Top: Mission Mountains by Mission Creek. GEORGE WUERTHNER
Right: Western Grebe at sunrise. KEITH SZAFRANSKI

Top: Beartooth Pass.
GEORGE WUERTHNER
Left:Fall color along the Yellow-
stone River below Yankee Jim
Canyon; north of Corwin Springs.
TOM DIETRICH

Facing page: The Pintlar Range
between Wise River and
Wisdom. RICK GRAETZ

Top: In the Absarokas looking at a rock glacier on the slopes of Emigrant Peak above Emigrant Gulch.
GEORGE WUERTHNER

Left: Blaine County, snowed in.
MICHAEL CRUMMETT

Facing page, top: Hutterite farm and wheat field at sunset near Conrad.
TOM DIETRICH

Right: Cottonwoods between Sidney and Glendive.
DEL SIEGLE

Facing page: Cabinet Mountains
Wilderness, A peak, Granite Lake.
PAT O'HARA

Top: Ninepipes Reservoir, Ronan.
KENT KRONE
Right: Bull elk and harem in Madison
River in Yellowstone National Park.
PHIL FARNES

9

Top: Lenticular clouds over the Crazy Mountains.
GEORGE WUERTHENER
Left: Fall on the Blackfoot River. RICK GRAETZ

Facing page: Wildflower field near Swift Current,
Glacier National Park. KENT KRONE

Facing page: Early winter in the Gallatin Canyon.
RICK GRAETZ

Top: Winter sunset in Big Hole Valley near Wisdom. GEORGE WUERTHNER
Right: Wild turkeys. MICHAEL FRANCIS

Top: Sky Top Lake Basin in the Absaroka-Beartooth Wilderness
PAT O'HARA
Left: Muskrat. CHRISTOPHER DWYER

Facing page: Scapegoat. RICK GRAETZ

Facing page: Kintla Lake,
Glacier National Park. DIANE
ENSIGN

Top: Glacier National Park,
view from Two Medicine Pass.
PAT OHARA
Right: Beaverslide hayrack in
Centennial Valley below the
Centennial Mountains.
GEORGE WUERTHNER

Top, left: Wildflowers in the Scapegoat. RICK GRAETZ
Top, right: Moonrise over Mount Harding, Mission Mountains and the Flathead Indian Reservation. MICHAEL CRUMMETT
Above: McDonald Valley, Glacier National Park. DOUG DYE
Left: Swan Range and the western boundary of the Bob Marshall. RICK GRAETZ

Facing page. Sunset off Flathead Lake Lodge on Flathead Lake. RICK GRAETZ

Above: Sky Top Creek in the Beartooth Range.
RICK GRAETZ
Left: Ptarmigan.
DOUG DYE

Facing page: The Big Hole River in Big Hole Valley by Wisdom.
GEORGE WUERTHNER

Facing page: Seeley Lake. RICK GRAETZ

Top:Looking at the Pintlar Range from between
Wise River and Wisdom. RICK GRAETZ
Right: Out on a limb, black bear cubs.
MICHAEL FRANCIS

Facing page: Chalk Butte.
JOHN REDDY

Top: Jewel Lake below
Mount Black in the Absa-
roka-Beartooth Wilderness.
GEORGE WUERTHNER
Right: Tobacco Roots south
of Sheridan. RICK GRAETZ

Top: Waterfalls in Hyalite Creek, Gallatin Mountains. JOHN REDDY
Left: August in the Madison Range. RICK GRAETZ

Facing page: Aspen-lined road in the Centennial Mountains. GEORGE WUERTHNER

Facing page: Barn on the west fork of the Bitterroot River. GEORGE WUERTHNER

Top left: Kerlee Lake in the Selway Bitterroot Wilderness. RICK GRAETZ
Top right: Indian Paintbrush. GARRY WUNDERWALD
Above: Fall on the Tongue River. RICK GRAETZ
Right: Blackfoot Valley. RICK GRAETZ

Top: Lima Peaks. RICK GRAETZ
Left: Snow ghosts at Big Mountain Ski Area near Whitefish.
RICK GRAETZ

Facing page: Terry Badlands. DEL SIEGLE

Facing page: Going-To-The-Sun Mountain, Glacier National Park. NEAL AND MARY JANE MISHLER

Top: Dawn on Harkness Lakes reflecting 18 Mile and Cottonwood Peaks, Beaverhead Mountains. GEORGE WUERTHNER
Right: Mallard hen protecting young ducklings at edge of pond. TIM CHRISTIE

Top: Flathead River near Bigfork.
RICK GRAETZ
Left: Cattle grazing below the
Blacktail Mountains near Dillon.
TOM DIETRICH

Facing page: Bob Marshall Wilderness, Prairie Reef. PAT O'HARA

Facing page: Redrock Lakes National Wildlife Refuge, Centennial Mountains. ROB OUTLAW

Top: Rocky Mountain Front and the Bob Marshall Wilderness near Choteau. RICK GRAETZ
Right: Mountain goat, Glacier National Park. BRUCE WEIDE

Top: Sunrise on Miller Mountain near Cooke City in the Gallatin National Forest. GEORGE WUERTHNER
Left: Tobacco Root Mountain Range and the Jefferson River Valley near Silver Star. RICK GRAETZ

Facing page: Snow-fields relecting on lake below Mount Allen. DIANE ENSIGN

Facing page, top: Little Chief Mountain in Glacier National Park. DOUG DYE
Below: Crazy Mountains east of Wilsal. RICK GRAETZ

Top: Elkhorn Mountains near Toston. RICK GRAETZ
Above: Fall leaves between Wibaux and Glendive. DEL SIEGLE
Right: Approching storm in eastern Montana. TIM EGAN

Top: Horses above Big Horn Canyon.
MICHAEL CRUMMETT
Left: Alaska Basin in the Redrock Lakes area.
GEORGE WUERTHNER

Facing page: Beargrass in the Scapegoat. RICK GRAETZ

Top: Greeting the dawn,
near Bozeman.
TOM DIETRICH
Left: The Sphinx.
RICK GRAETZ

Facing page: Alaska Basin,
Redrock Lakes area.
GEORGE WUERTHNER

Facing page: Fall color along East
Rosebud Creek near Roscoe.
TOM DIETRICH

Top: Custer National Forest near
King Mountain. JOHN REDDY
Right: Clark Canyon Reservoir, Lima
Peaks at sunset; south of Dillon.
TOM DIETRICH

Top: Cut Bank Creek Drainage, Glacier National Park.
DOUG DYE
Left: Northeast of Medicine Lake. RICK GRAETZ

Facing page: Tourquoise Lake in the Mission Mountains.
RICK GRAETZ

Facing page: Madison Range. RICK GRAETZ

Top: Horses at Bill's Place near Lima. GEORGE WUERTHNER
RIGHT: Fall in the Gallatin Canyon and the Gallatin River.
RICK GRAETZ

Top: Bannack. RICK GRAETZ
Left: Along the north fork of the Flathead River near Polebridge. TOM DIETRICH

Facing page: Fire in the Scapegoat Wilderness from Flint Mountain. RICK GRAETZ

Facing page: Mountaineer Peak in the Mission Mountains.
RICK GRAETZ

Top; Sunset over Chinook. RICK GRAETZ
Right: Mule deer buck. NEAL AND MARY JANE MISHLER

Top: Cow Island, Missouri River. RICK GRAETZ
Left: Paintbrush, aster, and groundsel among boulders along Zimmer Creek, Absaroka—Beartooth Wilderness. GEORGE WUERTHNER

Facing page: Smith River. RICK GRAETZ

Top: Bridger Mountain
Range. DEAN SAUSKOJUS
Right: Grizzley bear.
MICHAEL FRANCIS

Facing page: Square Butte.
RICK GRAETZ

Top: Swan River near
Bigfork.
GARRY WUNDERWALD
Left: Rocky Mountain Front.
RICK GRAETZ

Facing page: A prairie
falcon. LARRY THOMPSON

Facing page: 12,799 ft. Granite
Peak from Sky Top Lakes.
RICK GRAETZ

Top: Crazy Mountains.
DEAN SAUSKOJUS
Right: The Como Peaks in the
Bitterroot Mountains. TOM DIETRICH

Top: Avalanche Lake,
Glacier National Park.
GARRY WUNDERWALD
Left: Wildflowers in the
Hyalite Range. TIM EGAN

Facing page: Cow elk and
calf. MICHAEL FRANCIS

Facing page: Beartooth Mountains.
RICK GRAETZ

Top: Swan Range. RICK GRAETZ
Right: Great Blue Heron.
CONRAD ROWE

Top: Medicine Rocks near Ekalaka. RICK GRAETZ
Left: Springtime in Glacier National Park, Mt. Clements.
PETE AND ALICE BENGEYFIELD

Facing page: Rough Lake area in the Beartooth Mountains.
RICK GRAETZ

Facing page: Missouri River near
Cascade. RICK GRAETZ

Top: Big George Gulch, Rocky
Mountain Front. RICK GRAETZ
Right: Great Northern Mountain.
DOUG DYE

Top: Milk River wagon train.
MICHAEL S. CRUMMETT
Left: Holland Peak on the Swan Range.
RICK GRAETZ

Facing page: Soda Butte Creek, Yellowstone.
RICK GRAETZ

Top: Lupine below 18 Mile Peak, Beaverhead Mountains. GEORGE WUERTHNER

Facing page, top: Sunset on Emigrant Peak, Paradise Valley. GEORGE WUERTHNER
Right: Great Plains in spring near Glendive. GEORGE WUERTHNER

Top: Yellowstone River near Columbus. GEORGE WUERTHNER

Facing page: Glacier backcountry, Vulture Peak. RICK GRAETZ

Facing page: Lima Peaks in
the Beaverhead Mountains.
GEORGE WUERTHNER

Top: Going-To-The-Sun Road
in Glacier.
GEORGE WUERTHNER
Right: Flathead cherry
blossoms.
MICHAEL CRUMMETT

Top: White Rocks section of the Missouri River. RICK GRAETZ
Left: Canadian geese with young goslings. TIM CHRISTIE

Facing page: Beartooth Wilderness. RICK GRAETZ

Facing page: In the Beartooth
Mountains from the Beartooth High-
way. RICK GRAETZ

Top: Mount Edith, Mount Baldy and
Canyon Ferry Lake. JOHN REDDY
Right: Mount Harding in the Mission
Mountains. TOM DIETRICH

Facing page, top: Chinese Wall at the head of Moose Creek in the Bob Marshall
Wilderness. RICK GRAETZ
Left: Yellowstone River. RICK GRAETZ

Top: Between Bigfork and Somers. RICK GRAETZ

Facing page: Beartooth Mountains.
RICK GRAETZ

Top: Bull River Country. RICK GRAETZ
Right: Male mountain lion hunting for
prey. TIM CHRISTIE

Facing page, top: Bighorn rams outside Gardiner. MICHAEL CRUMMETT
Left: Smith River Canyon. CONRAD ROWE

Top: Big River Meadows and Gateway Pass in the Bob Marshall Wilderness. RICK GRAETZ

Top: Mount Merritt, Glacier National Park. RICK GRAETZ

Facing page, top: Missouri River. RICK GRAETZ
Right: Spanish Peaks. RICK GRAETZ

Top: The Sphinx, Madison Range.
JOHN REDDY
Left: Moose in Yellowstone National Park.
NEAL AND MARY JANE MISHLER

Facing page: Krutar Ranch, Blackfoot Valley near Ovando.
RICK GRAETZ

Top: Crazy Peak.
TIM EGAN
Left: Rocky Mountain Front,
Ear Mountain. RICK GRAETZ

Facing page: Looking to
the Gravelly Range, Ruby
River Valley.
GEORGE WUERTHNER

Top: Paraglider in Glacier. LISA HALE

Facing page,top: Silver Star Llama Ranch below Holland Peak. RICK GRAETZ
Right: From Bridger Canyon looking south.RICK GRAETZ

Top: Goat Lake, Selway Bitterroot Wilderness. RICK GRAETZ
Left: Centennial Mountains and Redrock River. JOHN REDDY

Facing page: Paradise Valley from Pine Creek Moraines along the front of the Absaroka Mountains.
GEORGE WUERTHNER

Top: Bull River Valley. RICK GRAETZ

Facing page, top: North Fork of the Flathead River. GARRY WUNDERWALD
Right: West of Cascade and the St. Peter's Mission area looking towards the Rocky Mountain Front. RICK GRAETZ

Top: Middle Fork of the Flathead River. RICK GRAETZ

Facing page, top: Hi-Line ground blizzard, -110 fahrenheit wind chill. MICHAEL CRUMMETT
Left: Highwood Mountains. RICK GRAETZ

Lower St. Marys Lake, Glacier National Park. DOUG DYE.